The crushed and voiceless ones will find
resonance in the broken drum
amplifying their cry for help.
Your call has been heard.
Hold on!
The oil of gladness waits to be poured out in
response.

These pages are for our friends who couldn't make this
journey...and for those yet to set out.
Be encouraged!
Keep listening to the one who allures us into the desert.
Do not be afraid...it is the place where He speaks.

OLD DRUM
NEW SKIN

as
journeyed by

David Baker & Nick Breakspear

Pilgrim Designs
44 Surrey Street
Millom
Cumbria
LA18 4LH

ISBN 978-1-5272-6099-3

Cover Design by Shooters Media.
Front cover photograph 'Old Drum'
by The House of John wet-mob-dancers Blackstone Edge
Back Cover photograph 'New Pow Wow Drum'
by The House of John wet-mob-dancers Blackstone Edge

'Old Drum, New Skin' is the joint enterprise of modern day explorers David Baker and Nick Breakspear. It journals their incredible adventure to an aboriginal gathering in Perth, Western Australia in 2011; a surreal exploit filled with unexpected 'highs and lows'.
Now, after nine years gestation, the foolhardy duo sense it is time to share their findings.
Oh - and by the way - it's got pictures.

Old Drum New Skin

What is this - I can see
It's a picture
It's a picture

It's a circle
Made of wood and leather
It's a transmitter
It's a receiver

Just an old drum that needed a new skin
So it could play, play again

Looks like it was made for gathering
Broken hearts together - Broken hearts together - like mine
Hey it's gathering... time

Nick Breakspear 2019

Foreword

So what's the weather got in store for us today, she asked reaching for her smartphone. A far cry from in my Grandma's day - when she would instinctively look up at the mucky brown sky and say "Brrrr - time to wrap up, snow is on the way"; and she didn't have a meteorological degree, just an ordinary woman 'tuned in' to her world.

What did she know?

How do people detect when something NEW is coming?
It's not an easy science.
Not always as simple as 'reading the clouds'.
How do we know when change is 'in the air'?
After all, we don't want to miss out do we?

What do you see?

Can we read the peculiar signs? The veiled way markers hinting at a different/alternative slant on life's journey; because there are many signposts vying for our attention; endless rivers of distraction; but these are not what we truly seek. These distracting fripperies will not take us 'home'. No, instead we yearn for those serendipitous, extraordinary seeds of inspiration camouflaged amongst the ordinary - hidden in sight, sound and story.

These precious nuggets lay dormant in the daily humdrum.... waiting to be sparked into life. Seeking to allure and engage us into a different kind of conversation.

Sound tantalizing?....Let's give it a go.
We did - and wrote a book about our offbeat experiences.

This is it.
Enjoy 'Old Drum, New Skin'

Coffee & Heartbeats

Let the beat begin...

Location: Frankfurt International Airport

Nick and Dave had managed to find a quietish corner in the hectic terminal, which turned out to be a comfortable spot to while away a few hours, waiting for their connecting flight back to the UK.

Slowly slurping their milky cappuccino's they began reflecting on the past two weeks exploits in Israel, where they'd been part of a film crew documenting an indigenous gathering of around 500 colourfully dressed First Nation peoples. These faithful believers had literally journeyed from the four corners of the earth; up to the 'Holy Land' to see the place where Jesus had walked. Everywhere they went, they sang and danced their sacred songs of devotion. It was, as our American cousins put it 'Totally off the Charts!'

Finishing up the last of their frothy dregs, the conversation quickly gravitated to the central pulse of this amazing gathering, which had clearly emanated from the North American Native Pow-Wow Drum!
Now it just so happens that Nick and Dave are both percussionists, so the drum attraction wasn't particularly a fresh

one, however their newfound focus was. They found themselves surprisingly drawn to the simplicity of the beats. Beats that spoke on a whole new level!!!!!

Normally you find that most drummers want to play loud complex rhythmic patterns, but on this occasion - these drummers were oddly being slowed down.
Slowed right down to a literal heartbeat.

Lub – dub
Lub dub
Lub dub
This is the sound of a steady beating heart.

The term 'Lub – dub' came from Nick's wife Anni, who was a senior staff nurse at a local hospital. She'd overheard Nick and Dave talking about the heartbeat and offered an important insight from her nurse training days. Her tutor advised when first learning to detect the regular heartbeat, one needed to listen for the sound generated by the audible pulsating tones of - 'Lub – dub' - It's the sequence of the blood entering and leaving the hearts chambers on its life giving cycle around the body."

An Old Drum - Dave's Story

... Continuing on the percussive theme Dave began to tell Nick about some old drums he'd been given a few years earlier:

'I must have mentioned to my dad how I was collecting different drums to play with various groups and he'd said there were some old drums in a cupboard, at the church in Plymouth he attended; "I'll ask if anyone wants them or if they can be given away", he said.

They weren't wanted and fairly soon Dave received 3 marching drums; two snares and a big bass drum that had belonged to the Church Lad's Brigade of a previous congregation occupying the building. He really enjoyed playing them. The bass drum in particular had its original old vellum skin producing a beautifully warm sound.

A year or so later, whilst visiting another church group in Birmingham, Dave met a young man called Ronnie who the church had recently rescued off the streets. Ronnie was keen on drumming but had nothing to play so Dave loaned him the big bass drum; he was well chuffed.
On a later visit back in Birmingham Dave asked how Ronnie and the drum were doing; sadly Ronnie had disappeared back onto the streets and the drum was being 'stored'; "maybe you should come and get it," they said.
It was a sad sight that greeted him as he went to collect the drum from this big old house. It lay at the bottom of the cellar steps, its delicate vellum skin savagely torn and its shell spattered in concrete and plaster; abused and abandoned.
Nick was becoming increasingly agitated.

3

"That's not right!!!"...Nick said abruptly...."Over the years I've spent hundreds of pounds on flight cases to protect my drums!"

This beautiful old drum, built to beat out a rhythmic call to the faithful and provide the bass foundation for a marching band, now lay beaten, literally, and neglected. It wasn't just tragic, it was criminal.
Maybe.... Just maybe... this drum could be rescued and restored.... To play again.... As intended.

The details of Dave's story had clearly upset Nick, but why should he feel so deeply the pain of an inanimate object. It was as if he`d been personally wounded by what he was hearing.
After all this was just a story... right?

A New Drum is Born

Dave's sad tale subsequently became the bedrock inspiration for Nick to pen the twelve-minute epic "Old Drum - New Skin". Curiously this lamentful story of inexcusable violence surprisingly contained an antidote of healing hope.
However, as with many creative exploits there first came a maturing period as the project bubbled away on the proverbial back burner for the next two years. Like a good stock, it produced more and more depth of flavour as the calendar pages turned.

Meet Gloria

Introducing Gloria

We first met Gloria Miller, a softly spoken Aboriginal lady, whilst filming a documentary with Shooters Media. It was at the afore-mentioned 2008 World Christian Gathering of Indigenous Peoples (WCGIP for short) in Israel. This encounter took place at the first gathering site in the picturesque holiday village of Ginnossar, a sprawling resort complex situated on the northern shoreline of Lake Galilee.

On the second day Nick took a long stroll through the leafy gardens, trying to gather his thoughts, as the day before he'd received the sad news that his father had died. Awash with conflicting thoughts, especially as he was the first-born son – a big part of him wanted to be at home with the rest of the family to mourn the passing of their Dad – but he had been given his Mother's specific blessing to stay – in a phone call she'd left him with this remarkable assertion –
"Do not think of returning – we will wait for you – you must stay and complete the task our Saviour has given you".

Wow – what words!

Still reeling from his Mums moving directive, Nick felt an unexpected tap on his shoulder – he gingerly turned around and was greeted by three Aboriginal ladies, one of whom was Gloria and she was holding a six-foot spear.

Understandably, a little unnerved by the spear toting delegation, Nick politely responded, "Err... Hello.... Can I help you? "
The spear-carrying lady introduced herself: "Hi I'm Gloria Miller... these are my friends – we're here at the WCGIP gathering, representing the Noongyar tribe of South Western Australia".
Nick sort of nods knowingly – not having a clue who on earth the Noongyar people are. Then she asks a deeply searching question: "Is there something you need prayer for"?
Nick tearfully blurts out – "Yes.... my Dad has just died"
Gloria tenderly replies, "We thought there was something... we could feel your pain".

"You can feel my pain?".

"What?" thought Nick –"Is this for real?"
Have these Aboriginal ladies been divinely sent to look after me – to listen to my heart?"

What a picture!

Strangers one minute – then divinely connected friends the next. A trio of earthly wanderers quickly becomes four – standing in a foreign field – upholding a `fellow pilgrims' burden in prayer.
Later I ask Gloria – "What's with the spear"?
"It represents who I am" she replied, "It's my prophetic calling – Arrowhead Ministries"
Arrowhead Ministries.... Nick ponders and my name is Breakspear?...could this be the start of something... he wonders?

I Have a Gift for You
Later we exchange emails, followed by no contact whatsoever for the next two years.

Then right out of the blue she pops up in the UK.... Asking whether she can visit?
A few days later our antipodean friend along with her English travelling companion Helen Anderson arrive in the UK and more precisely at Nick and Anni's home. Gloria makes herself comfortable, sitting cross-legged on their living room carpet in typical Aboriginal style; she then proceeds to rummage around in a small leather bag looking for something or other...muttering, "Mmmm I was going to give that one... to such and such a body..."

Inquisitively Nick catches a glimpse of Anni's curiosity... which equals his own nosiness...they're both politely straining to see what is inside the bag?

Helen nonchalantly smiles at them both, seemingly familiar with her friend's eccentric ways.... it was a reassuring kind of look, as if to say, "all will be okay".

Gloria straightaway emerges as if on queue from her searching and cryptically announces: -

> "I have a gift for you Nick
> .... That's if you want it
> .... But it's up to you
> .... You will only get one chance for this"

Nick looks across the room nervously at his wife Anni ... both of them...are very unsure what kind of gift is being offered here... mixed with the puzzling thought "do I really want to receive it?"

The gift she offered turned out to be a smooth varicolored stone that Gloria had personally carried all the way from a tiny island way, way down in the South Pacific. She had faithfully waited upon the Lord until this time to show her exactly who to gift it to and pass on its astonishing story about an Elizabethan sea captain by the name of Pedro Ferdinand de Queirós.

He had been royally commissioned by the Queen of Spain to find Australia. Nonetheless he actually became famous for not finding Australia but instead bumping into a little known island called Espíritu Santo on Pentecost Sunday in 1606. Here he made a prophetic declaration that "from this time on until the coming of Christ, the gospel would be preached from here to the South Pole and it would be known as the Great Southland of the Holy Spirit". De Queirós' adventure is seen as a clear fulfillment of Jesus's prophetic words on the Mount of Olives, to take His good news to the 'ends of the earth'. The island of Espíritu Santo and the government of Vanuatu continue to bear witness to both of these prophetic statements.

Nick's After Thoughts

Many years down the line as we reminisce over these uncommon events I can plainly see, that had I not received and pursued this 'symbolically-loaded gift' none of our subsequent Breakspear Inc adventures would ever have happened. There would have been nothing more to tell...but thankfully I did receive her gift and more importantly the gift of friendship ...one that would blossom and bear more unexpected fruit in the years to come.

The first fruit of this harvest was to produce a music video based on Gloria's gift of a stone entitled 'Stones from the Staircase.' In it we depict a pilgrim's journey from the ends of the earth back to the Source, the Mount of Olives – where Jesus spoke his farsighted words 2000 years ago. Words that were being mind-bogglingly fulfilled by these islanders and other indigenous folks from around the globe (returning like boomerangs) back to where it all began.

Come to Oz...

... she said

It was January 2011 and the new year snows were falling in northern England when Gloria rang from a blisteringly hot Perth; she was calling to share about a wonderful vision she'd had for the coming November. Her plans were impressive; to put on an International event called KAAL CORROBEREE 2011 - "Fan the Flames". Corroberee by the way is an old Aboriginal word that means "gathering".

The purpose of the KAAL event was to gather together the body of Christ in Australia and Papua New Guinea as well as a whole bunch of international folks from the nations. Its aim was to empower and encourage participants through closing the gap of separation between Aboriginal and Australian people, reconciliation, family unity and respect for genders and cultures. This would include lots of storytelling, 'yarning', singing and aboriginal dance.

Now Gloria is a "Big Hearted Lady" who genuinely desires to bring people together. Fired up by the vision, she eagerly began inviting lots and lots of folk to the gathering, including her own Noongyar people as well as a host of homegrown Aussies and international guests.

The possibility of a large gathering was starting to build for the Corroberee.

Old Drum New Skin

Energized by the expectation of high gate receipts - Gloria
proceeded to invite the Breakspear mob "in faith" to put together
a ten-man team that would include a six-piece worship band and
a four-piece camera crew to film the event. Her invitation was
extravagant - an all expenses paid trip for our team to play at
this Aboriginal gathering in Perth, Australia.... Wow!!
It sounded utterly fantastic - imagine being paid to fly all the way
to Oz for three weeks and play!

.... So what's the catch? .... Some might say

Anyway, enough of such negativity...we enthusiastically put
together our 'dream team' and got stuck into rehearsing a full
set of songs. Our central focus was the standout track "Old Drum
New Skin" based on Psalm 133's message of unity. However
to fully paint this picture - we needed to commission, at great
expense, the crafting of a native Pow Wow drum from the "Sweet
Medicine Drum Company" in Taos, New Mexico; this would prove
to be the key element for expressing the unifying heartbeat.

Incidentally - while we had lots of inspiration to own the drum,
we didn't actually have any cash to pay for it. And this item was
not going to be cheap. The final cost rose to just shy of £1,500.
.....err but that did include a bespoke flight case!

Yet amazingly it came in, little by little as individuals supported
it into being. Like the person who gave £100, after winning a
grocery store till receipt draw from Morrison's supermarket! We
were royally blessed, so we took these signs as conformation,
that we were doing the right thing - in the Lord's eyes.

Meanwhile we were stirred to create four fringed buckskin
pennants to hang on the four corners of the wooden drum stand.
Each of these banners contained verses of peace and unity from

Psalm 133 along with the date of the gathering. Our good friend and Pyrographer, Sheila Clay expertly burned these inscriptions onto the leather for us.

We had a strong feeling that these items would be gifted to key people at the gathering, for them to take back to their communities as "memory keepers" of this seminal occasion.

Following the arrival of our brand new - super-dooper - Pow Wow drum - we seized the opportunity to gather the band together for a professional photo shoot. This turned out to be a fun filled media event, providing lots of shiny pics for our Ozzy P.R. inspiring a springboard of creative video ideas which we intended to film once we'd arrived down under – all in all - we were buzzing!

What Could Go Wrong?

Nine months to prepare, seemed like plenty of time at first ...however as the calendar pages quickly turned the "dream teams" initial zeal began to diminish, especially when the promised "all expenses paid flights" failed to materialize.

Sadly one UK band member after another withdrew from the venture - citing family constraints or work commitments for pulling out. Then to top it all - Phil Jones, our last musician who lives in Canmore, Canada, couldn't get his visa permit in time.

To be honest this was hard news to take, especially as this was supposed to be a so-called faith mission...the growing uncertainty had led us all to question if this journey was right or not.

On a spiritual level (no pun intended) this perplexing situation seemed to be degenerating into some sort of Gideon-esque

master class in divine mathematics (Book of Judges 6.11)
Subtracting to multiply? Really??? ... This was a whole different
way of ciphering.... One we were not used to.
But how can the learners know better than the teacher?

As we fast approached the final month, ten became five.

The Corroberee dates loomed ever nearer...we were down to just
two drummers Nick and Dave ...and the possibility of our camera
guys – Cop and Sparky...plus techy Kath... but NO band.
No keys
No strings
No harmonic melody making things....
What was the Lord up to?

I mean
     ...What on earth can two drummers do?

Suddenly we were down to the wire.... truth be known we had
actually passed all the deadlines!!! Even though the heavenly
word we had received was unswervingly clear – "this is going to
happen"– we were becomingly increasingly unclear on just how.
Practically and realistically its likelihood seemed to be fast
draining away. We were facing the prospect of a nil result and
the dire consequences of such an outcome was beginning to
dawn on us.

          ...Were we deluding ourselves?

And if it died – as now appeared likely – how could we ever trust
again – how could we believe again?
Let's be really honest here
HOW COULD WE EVER TRUST GOD AGAIN FOR ANYTHING?
                    HOW?

Old Drum New Skin

Pre-mortem Email
Nick, absolutely livid with the prospect of its demise, sent Gloria a desperate email - describing his undisguised grief for the metaphorical expectation of a " Son of promise" that was fast turning into a "Still born".
(Transcript in open letter email)

Desperate Email

Hi Gloria
It was good to yarn briefly earlier on Skype, I was sad to hear the tiredness in your voice, obviously you've been going flat out, whilst we have to be wholehearted in what we do, we aren't supposed to carry the whole burden – so enjoy your food!
Before we go any further I would like to re-affirm the questions I asked [from the letter below] these are not meant in any way as accusations, we are not having a go at you personally but trying get understanding of this situation.
We continue to seek the Lord for your guidance and well being our Sis – Shalom Nick xxx

------------------oOo--------------------
-   Open Letter   -

Metaphorically speaking we've decorated the nursery so to speak, got the cot and pram etc made everything ready, and after nine months labour we seem to be now looking at a 'still born` in our midst! Heavy words I know!

But this is how I feel and where Dave Baker and I are at. We have done everything that God and man have asked of us, we have prepared and are ready to go and deliver what we believe to be the `prophetic declaration' He has given us to bring at this time, however we are sat here in the UK twiddling our thumbs.

So we need to ask some serious questions about this KAAL gathering in Perth.
Like `what went wrong' because we need to know what happened-we don't have the baby of promise, which begs the big question "can we ever trust ourselves to `try' for another?"
Because everything about this invitation seemed so right!
In all of this I'm not trying to lay blame at someone's `scapegoats' door, but to properly debrief the situation and find the truth of our and God's actions.

I have spent the past few days and nights churning over the events leading up to this moment, sieving through the debris of what's left.

Did we have it all so wrong?
Wrong in the respect, that we had put our trust in the `gate attendance' being our financial saviour to provide the finances to get us there, rather than the Lord - the inspirer and finisher of this whole vision, which also begs another big question. Was He or did we, all just get carried away on a huge creative fest of doing `spiritual stuff'?
Either this is right?
Or it isn't?
Reality check? Have we deluded each other and ourselves?

X Marks the spot? Is Perth the starting point for this final out pouring into the rest of the nations?
If not what happens to what has been prepared for such a time as this, I speak of these alleged prophetic statements like the `Pow Wow' drum and its journey along with the accompanying soundtrack and presentation of `Old Drum New Skin'. Also, the

film `Stones from Staircase', based on this whole prophetic South Pacific relevant story. Because we thought that these two key components were for this 'appointed time' (not an entertainment item), we can't change the dates that have already been printed on the leather pennants we made them to give to those men and women who would take them as envoys back to their lands representing the four corners of the earth as a `sign and a witness' to this `birth'.

I DON'T THINK SO - nobody wants last year's calendars, because they are `out of date' no longer applicable – the time has gone – dead and buried!

As I said earlier, I`m trying to get understanding on this – not speculation!
So if you have clarity from the Lord – Please let us know.
Shalom - Nick

Utterly exhausted at the end of this mournful day, Nick dejectedly dragged himself to bed, squeezing out a final epilogue on the day to his wife Anni " I'm going to unpack those bags tomorrow"; Anni sighed in unison followed by a consoling kiss and hug; reassured, Nick rolled over.... He could rest now...No more sleepless nights ...The vision was lost, the dream was - Dead; we just needed to bury it.

Dave Reflects
Religious people often talk of 'Waiting on the Lord' with such ease as if it takes little effort and certainly has no hint of struggle or anguish. And yet, waiting, particularly combined with relying on someone or something else, requires a good deal of emotional energy and trust. You increasingly find yourself plagued by growing armies of 'what ifs'.
What if you heard it wrong?'

'What if your trust was misplaced?'
'What if you just really wanted to believe – and made it fit?'
'What if... What if.... What if'

In this busy, 'stay active' world of instant answers and 'quick dry' solutions, waiting is not easy and not generally recommended. Why wait when you can have it now.
As the deadlines passed Dave got to the very practical place where he was running out of clean clothes as well as running low on patient energy; all of his remaining clothes were packed and all his residual energy was draining away. We needed to give up - or go - and even between these two options we seemed to be narrowing down to the one realistic choice: time to give up.
It was at this moment I wanted to burn our provocative T-shirts with the invitation to -

Be Realistic... DREAM

Tour T Shirt Logo

Shooters Media – Film crew reflections
Paul Coppack and Paul Sparkes a.k.a 'Cop and Sparky' were driving over to Rochdale the day before the fated deadline.
Here's a snippet of their 'light-hearted' conversation.

Cop said; "I remember lots of nervous laughter in the car, as we giddily teased each other about the unimaginable possibility – we could be on the other-side of the world in the next 24 hours. But how that was going to happen... was way beyond us."

Sparky humorously jested, "Yeah... Nick actually thinks he is going."

We both laughed!!!

Later we both puzzled; "had we known that this was really going to happen, we could have somehow found the cash. But, instead we are locked into Gloria's generous offer to pay our expenses – sadly though the money just didn't arrive."

Resurrection Call

7am the next day Nick's mobile starts ringing!!!

"Who on earth can this be...at this hour...no one rings me.... uh?"
"Hi Nick" a distant voice says...
"Uh!   ...David?"
It was David Clements, a visionary guy Nick had met six months previously at a friend's funeral in Bethlehem. They instantly hit it off. David is American by birth of Jewish and Native American descent. He is also an ordained minister, and a Vietnam veteran.

David immediately apologized for ringing at this hour, only now realizing that there was a two-hour time difference between the UK and Crete from where he was calling.
"Hey.... sorry man.... I'll call you back in a couple of hours...I've got a story for the storyteller...and it's all good!"
"Uh!"
"OK" said Nick, putting the phone down and returning soundly to his previous slumbers, without another thought, because it couldn't have anything to do with Perth - that vision was dead.

Dave Baker was due round at Nick's house later that morning, they wanted to unpack their cases and the death of the vision before making a start on the post mortem. When Dave arrived, Nick told him that he was expecting a Skype call from David Clements 'any time now' – and that he had a story for the

18

storyteller – But even then, they couldn't see how anything could alter the stark facts – it was over and there was no use kidding themselves otherwise. Curiously and quite perceptively - Nick had felt to break out his old mini disc recorder and set it up to tape the forthcoming conversation which turned out to be one of the most surreal and momentous 47-minute conversations they had ever been involved in – and it was all on tape (well disc).

The edited transcript highlights are below.

A couple of things to consider as you read them:

- Dave Baker had never met David Clements before and Nick didn't really know him that well either.
- David Clements knew very little about our situation and certainly none of the detail of what had brought us to this point in time.
- Repeatedly throughout the call Dave and Nick looked at each other with expressions that said: is this really happening, what is going on?
- Even as David seemed to rekindle hope we found it difficult to believe that anything could now happen
- Could the dead really be brought back to life
- And even if the dream was renewed how could this now happen – HOW?
- Behind the words there was a lot of nervous shuffling and laughter
- Somehow as the 47 minutes progressed, not only were we starting to believe –

  BUT
- It seemed that divine interventions were beginning to have their way

Skype Conversation 2011

What follows is a RAW transcript of the Skype conversation between David Clements (**David C**), Nick Breakspear (**Nick**) and David Baker (**Dave B**).

David C: So - what's up my friend

Nick: (laughs nervously) We're caught up in the enquiry.

David C: (also giddily laughs) You're caught up in the enquiry eh!

Nick: Yeah…. My mates here …Dave Baker

David C: - Hi Dave

Dave B: - Hi Dave – you alright

David C: Hi Dave … Dave isn't here! (David likes to be called by his full name David = "Beloved of Yahweh" in Hebrew)

We all laugh apprehensively!

Nick: like the communiqué I sent you says, we are trying to figure it all out! We've been ready and waiting for the past fortnight, but were just immobilized really, we couldn't do anything …mmmm anyway it's not materialized.
But it's like why is this…

David C: ya ya…. Well I'll tell you the story I was supposed to tell ya.

Nick: - Good… we're waiting!

David C: About five or six years ago, we had been travelling in the States for some time, doing ministry. It was a glorious time, sleeping on floors with the baby, being treated like royalty ...you know. This had gone on for quite some time. We had stopped in Hawaii and had the baby – we knew we had to go back to Israel, but nothing was coming together in the same way as you're having your problem. I had a number of people who stepped forward and said that they would help this way and that way. The offerings were just enough to get us from one city to another. I'm talking all the way from Hawaii completely across the United States by car.

Nick: "Huh" (grunts in acknowledgement)

David C: Until we had arrived in a mid-point somewhere in Texas I ran into a pastor who said" I can open up two or three churches to ya...we're gonna bless you.... provision will arrive." Then it turned out that he was somewhat of a charlatan!

Nick & Dave B: (let out a big laugh thankful for the lightening of mood)

David C: All of that stuff – ups and downs. Knowing that we were supposed to return to Israel and time was running out. The time on Katia's (David C's wife) American visa was running out, she had to go back to Israel (she was an Israeli citizen). We had to go back to Israel – but we didn't have to either – we could have stayed and I could have gotten her residency in the country. But no help was coming from anywhere...and everything in Israel that should have been receiving us like your guys in Australia... Nothing was happening. So we arrived at this point where we had a couple of hundred dollars. We were faced with transporting four people on the airplane. Then on top of that to be able to survive in the hostility of Israel.

Nick & Dave B: (let out another big chuckle)

David C: to be able to make ends meet there, it's a difficult area of ministry, as you well know. I would rather have gone to Vietnam to preach the gospel than Israel, just all of that stuff going on you know?   Nothing happened – here we are with a week or so to go – I had the tickets set up – but I can't pay for them. And the Lord leads me to read 1 Chronicles 29
There's this weird thing going on in 1 Chronicles 29 that I'd never seen before. King David was reaching the end of his days – the passion for the Lords house had never let him go. He was still consumed by a passion. You guys are in this passionate moment now.
Passion has produced a number of things – drums – banners – songs - all of this. So, David is consumed by passion for the house of God and he comes to this place where he just abandons himself and makes his own offering. The text says when you read through it "There was no offering made by any people – then David made an offering – then the princes of Israel made an offering – then the captains of ten thousand and the captains of a thousand they all made an offering." It was from this passion – not from the people – but from the passion of leadership that Solomon was then able to build the house.
David's offering was somewhere around 30 – 50 million dollars (in today's calculation) out of his own resources. I said - so Lord what are you telling me here...and he said
"There is no altar that you can approach that I do not demand a sacrifice."   ...I said Oh! The higher the calling the bigger the sacrifice - David." I said - so what do you want me to do Lord? He said "Sell everything you have and make your own sacrifice – and let it be a witness in the eyes of all men – what you do." So I sold it all – I sold the car - I stripped us down of all that we had - I sold it all. Because of the one thing that I could be sure of was "that the call was real". That the alignment of the finances

wasn't the reality – it was the call! And the passion of that call – the passion towards His house – the passion towards His people. I realized that when Elijah built that altar – he forfeited his very life – for if the Lord hadn't answered by fire – it would have killed him. So, he stepped all the way into it. I realized that as a Jew there was no way that you could approach the Lord without conforming to his order – and that his order demanded blood and sacrifice – burning flesh. I determined that should I perish along with my family – I would follow my passion.

So, we sold everything – it was interesting the way God did it – I had a coin that I found in Israel whilst sweeping the yard that supplied the airline tickets. And other things that gave us the ability to live. The most unusual thing that happened when we got there (Israel) was that no believer helped us. Nobody in the church or anything. But some orthodox Jews who we knew gave us their apartment to live in Beth Shemesh –(House of the Servant) the city where the Ark of the Covenant stopped. It was from that we launched out and where we stand now is all based on that. Everything we are doing now in the nations is based on that.

The Lord told me "His way was that it would've come from another direction". The sacrifice, the ability to do what we are doing. That there was disobedience in place and that there was something that wasn't right in people. That they didn't do what he had told them – So He said, "You do it"; so, we did.
He told me I'll take you on a journey where everything will unfold as you move. The steps of the righteous are ordered of the Lord But not the 'standing' of the righteous but the 'steps' of. And that happens to this very day. When I saw you (at the funeral) I had left my family in Crete on my crazy journey through Italy and Switzerland and all that. I had 150 euros in my pocket and my wife had 175 euros here when I left. The journey continued

to unfold; with three and a half weeks of work/ministry in all these different nations. I returned home with 6,000 euros, which came from the most unlikely of sources. Someone walking up and said "I want to pay for all your plane tickets to Scotland and Ireland and your car – here's the money. Some man walked up in a meeting in Germany and said, "No longer will you pay for plane tickets. I will pay for all of your travel in the future – just send me your time and dates – and I will take care of you – I'll arrange your tickets from now on."

Had I not gone - none of the lives would have been touched, none of the people would have been ministered to. None of the young people would have gotten their passions restored or found.

It would probably take a book on this last trip to record how many people emailed and said, "My life has been altered and changed." So, the walk remains the same. I wake up – I climb up onto a 30-meter diving board (metaphorically speaking), blindfolded, standing on the end, praying that there is even water in the pool...

Nick and Dave B: (chuckle nervously: again)

David C: ...and again; I dive. Somewhere in this crazy story is hidden what you should do.

Nick and Dave B: (chuckle again)

Nick: Yeah that was nervous laughter.

David C: (laughs too) I don't think it's too hidden.

Nick: No it ain't ! (in-between choking)

David C: What I hear very clearly is it doesn't matter what it takes ....get on the plane and go.

Old Drum New Skin

Nick: assuredly says "Yeah"

David C: and the Lord will manifest everything that you have need of in abundance through your movements. You build an altar to His heart brother, and if you would find your life now; just loose it.

Long Silence Followed

David C: Because what He has called you to do and what He has given you is not a mistake and it's not for some other time It's not for banners to be mailed (this was a reference to the email and trying to make it fit). It's not for things to be kept. It's to die...ha-ha!

Nick: Thanks.... Ha-ha...yeah it's the truth though.... It's the truth...

Lots of squealing laughter and chortling from everyone.

David C: Though you know in your heart brother that you must go do this, He gave you a fire and a flame within, He chooses others to open their hand ...yet they can't brother; because they are the drum. They are the ones, who are battered and beaten and knocked from pillar to post. They cannot in their broken conditions always respond, and yet if you raise a man up from out of the ditch – He'll never forget you.

Nick: (gasps at the profundity of what is being presented) Your pulling them out of the fire this morning aren't ya!

Both David C & Dave B laugh in response

David C: I guess so

More undisguised laughter

Nick: You're such a blessing mate... I mean we've been racking our brains. Are we totally deluded with all this stuff? We've been back and forth over the whole process because we want reality; His reality! If we've blown it then we want to recognize that, but what we don't want is just to have another lumpy carpet and act like...Oh well ...that's it. But that's just crap and we are just being robbed.

David C: The blessing is equal to the resistance brother.

Long stunned silence followed by more unbelievable gasps!

Nick: (makes incoherent screeching tyre noises) Traffic cop

David C: If you would dream the dream then wake up from the nightmare friend. Step into the dream. It's a thousand meter drop and when you stick your foot over the open air brother, there a path will appear.
I told some people in Germany. "The Lord gave me a word to stand on this mountain to stand before Him every month and I will do it if all of you go and sit somewhere else. I will do it: I will respond. No matter the cost because He is worthy, He is worthy! So, I will fulfill the suffering of the cross that I might know the power of the resurrection but not I live, but that Christ lives."
Pay the price. You'll receive the reward brother and its souls.
If that gate is as critical as Gloria and others believe it is then to approach the altar that sits within that gate will be no easy thing.
All of creation is waiting for the mature sons of God and his daughters to appear.

Romans 8 reference – Nick and Dave bemusedly look at each other as if to say "was the Lord actually talking to us?"

Nick: You've just re-contextualized and reconfigured our understanding. Just before you came on, we were just discussing the whole thing about why we were not offered the option of paying for ourselves to go. From the beginning it was their invitation do it this way. In that sense we were immobilized as not being in the equation. We're still immobilized... cause we ain't got the cash. Hahahaha but what your saying is beyond the reality of having it in your hand (Sweaty mitt).

David C: Well Nick I had a distinct feeling this morning, when I was calling you earlier. I read one email from you last night and I got stirred a little bit, then I started calling you with this. It wouldn't let me go I just kept walking round the house over it. I like how you changed that front-end lyric about - Taking the clock off the wall
"Take down the wall clock it's really messed us all up"
(He was referring to the new version of Old Drum New Skin)

This is or was all about KAIROS

There are certain things that the Lord is doing in that region that he can't do unless he puts men to the test. So, he stays His hand until the moment that he can move forward. He never judges a man unless he tests a man. He only judges to bring alignment and order. Its all a part of what is going on in that region; in that gate. There's a lot of stuff moving down there. It all comes to this moment; the real 26th hour.

Nick: (dejectedly says) It really is because we physically can't get there now.

Nick to Dave B: Can we?

Dave B: I don't know, we need to check it.

Nick: Yeah...we will check it but err!!

Everyone bursts into nervous laughter

Nick: The times that I'd looked at previously to get there for tomorrow, to be there for Saturday really.

Nick rambles on about the permutations of flight times

David C: (cuts straight through) Well maybe this is one of those times we pray - God Speed.
This is met with everyone bursting into nervous laughter

David C: Maybe you should look around for someone to baptize when you get finished. ...You'll just be in Australia.

Dave B: Phillip... I don't know?

David C: Maybe there's an Ethiopian eunuch somewhere?

Dave B: You never know

Nick: Probably in this neighbourhood yeah!
(David was referring to another dreamy event in the New Testament, Acts 8.26)

David C: Well I don't know how it's all going to play out but if your hearts have been turned this way, which I feel it has, that's the critical matter. That there's no waste in what God has given you.

Nick asks David C if he has seen the film (Old Drum New Skin)

David C: No (he hasn't clicked on to it yet)

Nick: Cause it just adds to the madness.

David C: The other thing is this. If you don't get there, you weren't supposed to be there. It doesn't mean that anything you did was wrong. Maybe there are some things aren't moving and shifting right in that region, for the Lord to release this, completely release it right now. It's just that there are a lot of pieces and parts of this in the spirit that you cannot see. The only thing you can see is your heart.

A pause hangs in the air

David C: and its right

Nick: Well we've checked and re-checked and all that, and we feel everything's "Kosher"

David C: It is ...it is

Nick: Thank you for the banquet you've laid on.

David C: (laughs acknowledgingly) You are very welcome. I realise it was a bit of a steak but I knew you could handle it.

Nick: Yeah...well we've come this far...and everything has died ...I think. So we are looking for resurrection, whatever it means, you know. We still ain't unpacked; we are ready to go you know.

David C: Be cracking bro ...there maybe something moving tonight.

Nick: Yeah?.....I think so ????

Lots more nervous laughter from the musketeers

David C: All right I'll leave you be. Keep me posted alright?

Nick: Will do mate.

David C: Love you brother - Nice meeting you David.

Dave B: Nice to see you David.

David C: You too brother.

Nick: Thanks for waking us up.

David C: Your welcome Nick.

Nick: I mean that in the real sense you know.

David C: thanks for letting me ...Love ya brother.

In 4 Hours

Following on from this astonishing conversation.
Dave and Nick not real sure how to proceed ...stood up and prayed...
"OK Lord you've got our attention ...what's the story.... we are ready to hear!"

As soon as they had finished praying Dave had an out loud thought:
"...Mmm I think my salary goes in today, maybe I've got enough for a flight. I need to get to an ATM and see!"
"Good for you" Nick said sarcastically.
So we drove into the local town. Dave found a branch.
Exiting the bank he joyfully exclaimed, "Hey I've got enough!"

Nick scratched his head and suddenly remembered a little savings account he hadn't used for some time ...I wonder if...let me have a look...

Within four hours - we had the funds – amazingly a flight was found – seats were booked - and we were on our way to Manchester airport.

But first we had to make a quick phone call to Gloria to explain the sudden turn around.
"Hi Nick where are you"

"We are on our way" replies Nick, which was met with great jubilation "England is coming ...England is coming..." Gloria cried!

We urgently needed Gloria to process the official paper work for the drum to gain access into the country through its vigorous bio-security. Without this key document being accepted, the drum would either not be allowed into Australia or quite possibly destroyed!!!! (Was this yet another test?)
Also we had a problem with taking our drum stand as it was heavy and its raw wood would not clear Australia's customs. It wasn't going to make the trip, so we asked Gloria if someone in Oz could make one.
Her good friend Vanda had a son who was a carpenter and he would produce a fine stand for the drum for when we arrived.

Just before boarding the plane Nick made a final quick call, this time to "Shooters Media" to let the camera guys, Cop and Sparky, know what was happening - Cop actually thought that we were ringing him to say - get down to the airport, we're off – Nick was so impressed with their level of faith, especially as so called non-believers - to be willing to drop everything and come...but sadly the finances didn't stretch to five and for them this adventure was not to be. Thankfully they've been able to join us since – filming further Breakspear Inc escapades.

At 20:10 that evening we took off from Manchester UK on our Emirates flight to Dubai; this was the first leg on our way to Perth.
29 ½ hours later we arrived in Australia

At 2:00am on Saturday November 27th we arrived at Perth International airport.
After 2 hours of tense form filling with Bio Security, the all-important `drum permits' were accepted - to our great relief.

Nevertheless the Border guards took a dislike to 4 of our Pow Wow beater sticks and ceremoniously confiscated them (more form filling in triplicate ensued). Finally the Australian authorities gave us the all clear to enter their land with our now `Kosher' Abba drum.

It was 4am ...time to load the car and head for the Corroboree campsite and our first bed...Zzzzzz

Timing is...

...everything

It had only been two weeks prior to the event that the Lord impressed upon Nick that the KAAL gathering was going to be for us a Kairos moment, `an appointed time', when `He` was going to open a doorway into His divine purposes. Wow this was starting to sound like a most intriguing adventure ...one that Dave and Nick were definitely up for.

Perhaps a better way of describing Kairos, can be seen in the saga of the children of Israel going round and round in circles for forty years in a seemingly endless wilderness– after which they were offered access into the `Land of Promise`. They had `one chance for this' - a loaded phrase very reminiscent of Gloria's words to Nick when she cryptically offered him a stone from a remote beach on Espiritu Santo. Just like Israel if they hadn't taken what was being offered them in their Kairos moment they'd have had to stay on `Chronos /wall clock time' going round and round all over again.

Naturally speaking the Breakspear mob were supposed to have been in Perth at least a week before the beginning of the festival; however the Lord had made it clear to us in prayer - saying that our part in this gathering would be at the end - on the last day - He was very specific!

Last Spot on the Last Night
So finally here we are... X marks the spot. We have arrived at the

KAAL festival ... about to deliver what the Lord had given us to bring from the other side of the planet.

Nick had ruthlessly cut down the presentation to a single track, the one and only `Old Drum New Skin` followed by a screening of "Stones from the Staircase" a short film we had produced, inspired by Gloria's stone gift to Nick.

Rubber time:
The finale was scheduled to start at 7 0'clock, however after much munching on their local delicacy – roasted Kangaroo tail - folks gradually arrived about 8ish, now the evening's programme could get underway.
However unbeknownst to us the site management had pre-imposed a 10 0'clock curfew on the PA sound system, which had the potential to cast a dark shadow on the last night's fun.

The time was fast approaching 9:55 when suddenly Breakspear Inc was introduced as the last spot on the last night.

Bring the drum:
Earlier in the afternoon we had commandeered 3 extra drummers from the PNG (Papua New Guinea) mob, as they like to call themselves, to join our UK mob, as we like to call ourselves. Because of numerous technical difficulties we couldn't get to rehearse with them and the soundtrack, which we felt quietly at ease about, after all this was real time - not a rehearsal.

Dave Baker and the PNG guys were situated at the back of the gathering with the Pow Wow drum lifted high on their shoulders - each of them wearing miners' helmets complete with T-shirts that read "Be Realistic – DREAM". The drum was covered in a bloodied white sheet, the house lights had been cut, so the only light in the huge agricultural barn was eerily coming from the lamps on the lads' miners' helmets.

Our pre-recorded soundtrack began to fill the air with lamentful notes as we set off like a sad funeral procession, swaying and wailing through the gathering - sorrowfully ever onwards towards the awaiting drum stand placed at the foot of the stage. As the drum bearers moved, their headlamps flashed and spilled onto the faces of those gathered within, momentarily giving light to their darkened silhouettes.

At the head of the procession was Nick, wearing a radio head mic, complete with stethoscope and matching blue hospital scrubs with the same "Be Realistic Dream" logo printed back and front - he proceeded slowly forward with his arms open wide, like a modern day prophet striding into the wilderness, declaring the opening lament:

"I found me an old drum, it got a broken skin"

The four drummers followed behind carrying the huge drum in mournful unison. Our sorrowful band processed through the crowd, accompanied by the dramatic soundtrack, which was progressively increasing in volume. Finally they landed just before the main stage, unloading the drum onto its awaiting wooden stand where they removed the bloodied sheet and laid it on the floor. Despite the lack of rehearsal time their movements were sensitively tuned in to the drama of the moment as it unfolded through the soundtrack and it's graphic lyrics.

The four now face the drum, its skin illuminated by narrow beams of light emanating from their helmets. A split second of sacred stillness falls - before they reverently pick up their beaters and begin to play the opening heartbeats on this precious Abba drum.

Suddenly the atmosphere changed as Nick proceeds to sing the
next verse.

> He moves heaven and earth
> To show His hands of love
>
> He moves heaven and Perth
> To show His Hands of love

Nick has a split second unspoken thought "Perth...we`ve
arrived!"

Unexplained and unannounced Nick picks up a 4-litre can of
virgin olive oil which was waiting for him at the side of the stage,
removing the cap he lifts the container high above his head and
begins to pour out the golden juice, tenderly wooing the oil with
these lyrics.

> Oh my love my beautiful broken and battered ones
> Come away...Come away with me...
> To my Gethsemane ...come away

Nick continued singing and pouring the can of oil from on high...
when all of a sudden and without invitation - PNG Pastor Andrew
rushed forward and began to seize the gushing oil - Gloria saw
it too. Then another. And another came running - It was as
if the people wanted to access the lavish heart of Psalm 133 -
triggering a torrent of emotions - tears and laughter – we didn't
know whether the oil was cascading down - or erupting.
It was like a wellhead fountain splashing and soaking everyone in
its profound mystery.

For a few seemingly timeless minutes, we reveled in divine
mayhem. All this was happening as Nick continued to sing his

version of psalm 133.

> How good and pleasant it is when Brothers and Sisters
> Dwell in unity
> It's like oil poured down
> On the head
> On the feet
> Of those who hear His heart beat
> For there the Lord commands
> He commands a blessing
> Forever and ever more

STOP!!!!!!!!!!!!!!!!!!! A voice rang out!!! Suddenly the house lights went on, causing everyone to gasp, squint and cry....
NO!!!

Visibly shocked by the sudden splash of unwelcome brilliance the gathering now understandably was rubbing their eyes.
Yet as we adjusted our focus - the room revealed a crowd of oddly dazed looking folk - some laughing - others in tears - individuals staggering to stand upright - as if drunk – others had already made it to the floor.

The ecstatic rare moments experienced only a few seconds ago, had been abruptly brought to an end by Danny the sound engineer... tapping the sound desk mic for our attention.

Standing next to Danny was an officious looking site manager... his face red as thunder!

He was here to uphold the curfew - agreed some days earlier - apparently after noise complaints were brought by a number of the campsite's neighbours.

As was earlier mentioned – Nick and Dave were totally unaware of the 10pm curfew which had been imposed by the site management – so was it any wonder that the "flock were going to get some flack" by inviting Breakspear Inc to start their 12-minute track at 9:55.

Of course it was a heavy handbrake blow on the nights finale, but one that proved to be a sobering `reality check` to the gatherings heavenly aspirations.
Nick reminded the gathered that we are supposed to be good neighbours ...saying that he "liked good neighbours.... and wanted to be one too".

But not all was lost...
We still had our short film "Stones from the Staircase" to show, but only if the volume was turned right down ...so we asked engineer Danny... who obligingly tweaked the volume controls from eleven to more acceptable decibel levels.

We encouraged everyone to draw closer to the screen, and they happily complied...not a murmur was heard.... making the whole experience even more intimate and intense.

After the screening the leaders of the gathering collectively prayed and thanked us for making the arduous journey all the way from Olde England to bring them this well-timed oily message of unity. Followed by lots of hugging and sharing of gifts, which included our very own offerings, Psalm 133 - buckskin pennants.

Our assignment was done, but the ripples continued....

The significance of what had taken place was that the Lord

had truly opened up a gateway to a `healing fountain of reconciliation'.

Throughout the next day individuals young and old spoke of personal healings, some accounts given through translators, many still glowing with mystified expressions unable to fully articulate what had happened - being totally awed by the unforeseen happening. Stories emerged of the youth group, who had returned in the middle of the night to lie down on the bloodied white sheet, soaked by this oily wellhead. Their intention was to get closer to the presence of God.... wanting more of Him. There was no need for further testimonies ...the faces that glowed before us ...said it all.

And this was just our first night in OZ...

...But the Lord had lots more in store.

As David Clements put it... "The reward... is equal to the resistance"

Nick's backstory to Psalm 133
Over the months leading up to this moment, Nick kept getting an image in his mind of Psalm 133 and its flowing oil message of unity, he had a euphoric feeling that at some point during this song, oil was to be poured over the head of an Aboriginal leader. (He wasn't sure at all how this was going to work out).
Earlier in the day Nick had asked if someone could get him some olive oil and leave it near the foot of the stage – they did - but he got quite a surprise when he saw that they had actually purchased - a 4 litre can...maybe the Lord wanted to show us what he really means by being LAVISH?

This was truly an extravagant amount...definitely not something to be stingy with.

Dwelling Up

Day two in Oz....
What a landing - we reflected. We tried to catch our breath; still reeling from Saturday nights amazing events.

The two Poms quickly turned their thoughts to the week ahead and wondered what would fill the blank pages of their diary. They didn't have to wait long for a reply.

 A few moments later Gloria popped in to ask us if we would be interested in sharing our story with other groups in different places. "Yes please" we replied..."this is was what we've come for".... so Gloria made a few calls and we prepared to head off on fresh adventures. Joining us on this journey would be Gloria's friend Warren a fellow Noongyar with his own tale to tell.

So we loaded up the car and trailer and drove inland for several hours, eventually arriving at a place called Dwellingup, a small sleepy town, in a timber and fruit-growing region of the Darling Range, east south east of Pinjarra.
Dwellingup is a remote and scattered community in a dark Jarrah forest, with less than a thousand residents. We arrived at a newly renovated colonial style house with a large wrap-round veranda, where we were introduced to a welcoming and hospitable family who fed and watered us royally as we waited for others to arrive. We soon began to trade stories – but more in-depth yarning would have to wait awhile as this house wasn't our final meeting

place; we would shortly be travelling deeper into the forest.
We also became increasingly intrigued by the name "Dwellingup"
- Was this another heavenly ambush that we were being allured
into?

The forest was dotted with idyllic looking 'holiday home' style
lodges each surrounded by allotments of self-sufficiency.
Pulling off the forest road we drove down a long winding
driveway, until we arrived at the rear of a beautiful two story 'A'
framed house.

As we exited Gloria's car it was immediately obvious that we had
entered one of nature's luxurious expressions, the air thick with
a tangible peace, as exotic birds called out from the canopies
above.

Here we were introduced to more new friends who had given up
their home for the night.
Feeling like a proper pair of blessed Poms, pinching ourselves,
we unpacked our gear including the treasured Pow Wow Drum.

As we unpacked the drum, setting it on its heavy wooden stand,
it attracted particular attention from a young couple called
Kirsten and Jesse. They began to share with us how they were
soon to leave Dwellingup feeling a call to the Southwestern
States of America, drawn to the indigenous peoples of that area;
uncannily the same region that our drum originated from.

The Pow Wow Drum seemed like a sign for them - and
increasingly for us.

The couple approached Dave as he was placing the beaters on
the drum skin, and expressed a desire to play and soon light
conversation gave way to soft intimate heart-speak-beats.

Old Drum New Skin

Jesse and Kirsten gazed at each other across the gathering drum; Dave quickly realized that this was their moment - just for these two, and he stepped aside.

The two now alone grooved a brand new rhythm of their own making, which wafted across the room drawing family and friends to acknowledge the sound of something fresh being birthed

Even before the meeting had formally begun, a growing sense of anticipation misted the air.

After a buffet meal with lots of yarning the meeting formally began.

Midnight Oil

Gloria shared with the gathering what had happened at the Corroberee and in particular about the pouring of the oil.

Nick seemed uncharacteristically reserved - not wanting to build up expectations or assume that we possessed some super-mystical blessing formula.

We simply gave a brief account of our dreamy journey so far, involving Psalm 133 and the oil.
The evening was getting late and understandably folks had to leave, after all it was a Monday night; they had jobs and school in the morning.
As numbers thinned out, we were left with a core group of around twelve.

Nick spied the can of olive oil and also the Axminster carpet underfoot and suggested we take the meeting outside.

The still night air was heavy with the sweet aroma of sun-toasted eucalyptus, as we walked out onto the lawned area. Instinctively we made a circle, just a bunch of modern day disciples standing in unity under a moonlit star-filled sky. We weren't really sure what might happen next but at the very least we knew we could pour out olive oil and recite the psalm of unity.

Moments of quiet reflection fell upon those gathered until interrupted by an elderly ladies fervent prayer of intercession: -

"We have been praying thirty two years for reconciliation with the Noongyar people"
Her eyes fixed on Gloria and Warren – both of them from this particular aboriginal tribe –
"But tonight is the first time they have been represented in our midst".

Struggling to remain upright...she cried out to the Lord with many tears, and heart-wrenching prayers of repentance for the historical atrocities committed in nearby Pinjarra. She was joined by others from the community in a deluge of sobbing as their collective sorrow flowed towards their now present aboriginal brother and sister. It was as if the Lord would not allow us to proceed without cleaning house.

In response Gloria and Warren extended their forgiving arms, visibly modeling Jesus` words "That they all might be ONE." After what seemed like a very long time the wailing ceased, oil was poured, the Psalm sung and the Creator's peace tangibly descended. Dave and Nick just stood there - open mouthed at this unexpected breakthrough – which clearly pre-empted Psalm 133's call for unity.

Spontaneously erupting into joyful songs of praise and prayers of astounded thankfulness - our eyes turned to the Makers star filled firmament at the wonder of what had just taken place; now with tears of laughter we began our "goodnights" to our newfound friends (just as it says in the Psalm).

Finally, around midnight with all but our small travelling band departed, we clambered into our beds - to the strains of Momma Gloria reminding us we had to be leaving around 5am for another long journey to Margaret River.... Happy days!

Road to Margaret River

Still buzzing from the night before everyone was up at 5am - just enough time for a quick swill and a brew, before hooking up the trailer to hit the long road south.
Stopping off at Bunbury beach for a proper breakfast, sufficiently suffonsified we continued on route 10 towards Margaret River.

The area is a well-known tourist destination brimming with beaches, wineries and craft breweries, however on the week of our visit, it was sadly overwhelmed by forest fires.
Margaret River, it turned out, had been the source of the smoke we had seen on day one, drifting across the International airport in Perth nearly 300 kilometers to the north.
Our reason for making the long journey south however was none of the above; we were here to visit a friend of Gloria's called Caroline.

Still heading south the fuel gauge was telling us to fill up soon; as we still had a good way to travel. We pulled off the main highway onto the backroads in order to find a gas station. Gloria happened to comment how nice it would be for us Brits to see some kangaroos "seeing as you're in Australia" she giggled.
So we're traveling along this tar road about forty to fifty miles an hour when to our delight Gloria's hope was realised... up ahead a kangaroo hops out right in front of us and follows the course of the road.
On the left,
On the right,
Happily hopping along in the middle of the road.

We slow down to watch - cameras at the ready. The Roo is clearly aware of us now and occasionally looks back to see how close we've come.

Slowing down even more - he stops - and moves inquisitively closer.

The Roo has a good look at us then hops off to the other side of the road and finally disappears into the bush.

"Wow" says Gloria "that was really special. Usually they're scared of cars and escape as fast as they can. Kangaroo road kill is a big problem around here. But he genuinely seemed to want to watch us. You guys have been blessed."

Twelve months on Nick was re-telling the tale of this unexpected sighting in a Sunday morning service relating his upset at how alien we have become to nature.

The majority of our contact with Gods good creation is invariably seen when our cultures clash.

The animals know the ancient ways, "the wild-invisible-tracks" but when they come into conflict with mans unyielding tar-road highways the result is far too often known as "Road kill" as if this was acceptable and sadly inevitable.

This "out there" thought also had a disturbing parallel in a lot of our church services, where we talk about being free 'Lifting up our hands or laying down to worship or dancing like David danced with abandon.'

Rarely is this passionate out-pouring actually seen in our "Chronos" time tabled meetings.

Sometimes we are so focused on our straight line narrow path ways of thinking that we fail to appreciate the cross cutting wild tracks of 'the Holy wind that blows where it will.'

How often is there room at the inn for the genuinely creative, the bounding kangaroo, the expressive believer to be free in our A to B...OHP led tar roads of controlled praise and worship?

Don't miss the scenery folks...it's all around us ......just waiting to be seen?

Warp and Weft – the wisdom of weaving?

After all you can't have the warp without the weft, but it appears that institutional thinking only wants straight up and down.

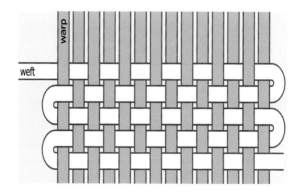

Zarephath

From the bush to the lush suburban gardens of Margaret River, we finally arrive at our destination. Turning into the grass verged pathway we drive past a stone building into the rear of the plot that opened out into an Olde English style garden loaded with well-tended blossoms and blooms. Gloria's friend Caroline, a quintessential English lady, wearing a floral cotton dress, is waiting and softly says hello and offers us a welcoming cup of tea with homemade biscuits and fruit. She politely ushers us towards the comfy seats situated on the shaded veranda of the ageing wooden chalet.

We all straightaway make ourselves at home to enjoy this delightful treat. Soon our conversation progresses, when we begin to understand that Caroline actually lives in this simple yet beautiful chalet in the garden and this is shortly confirmed when she asks us the question "Do you want to see the house" and proceeds to walk us back up the drive to the entrance, where a brand new stone built bungalow was under construction.

Caroline tells us about the prevalence of forest fires in this region and how a simple change in wind direction can take a small hamlet or even a whole town by surprise. Even as we were there forest fires were raging in the distance and we had smelt the smoke as far away as Perth. Some years previously Caroline's house had been totally destroyed by fire leaving just its concrete base. This was not uncommon and the usual response was to clear the foundations and simply build again. Caroline however had heard a different voice: instead of rebuilding for herself she had felt to move into the garden chalet and build this new house - for God. Living simply she invested any spare funds in this project and it was definitely taking shape.

Caroline gave us a tour.

On solid foundations the external walls had been built and the roof was on, but internally none of the walls were in place; all we could see were wires and pipes waiting to be encased. Caroline excitedly mapped out the floor space - this will be the kitchen, bathrooms here, dormitory over there - and this will be the worship area. By now our eyes had been drawn to the walls defining the worship space. Caroline explained how she'd found a local firm that made these compacted concrete blocks - and they looked just like the limestone blocks of Jerusalem. The whole place was stunning.

Questions raced through our minds - where would people come from, who would come to worship here, when would it be finished and where would the funds come from. As if anticipating this last unasked question Caroline explained that currently funds had run out to which Nick surprised himself by asking if we could pray.

Nick turned to Dave and said, "Have we got any oil left?" Dave replied "I think there's a drop" and Nick answered, "that's all we need".

On hearing our oil conversation Caroline asked us not to pour it in the main room as she intended to create a decorative polished concrete floor finish, so we re-located ourselves to the doorstep entrance, seating Caroline on an old wooden stool overhanging the threshold as she'd recently had surgery on her hip - the rest of us stood outside. We prayed for this amazing lady and the worship centre as we dribbled the small amount of oil over her aged hands and the threshold, pouring it out until there was nothing left. Nick began to pray for this house of prayer...but suddenly to his surprise and everyone else he exclaimed out loud "This is a Zarephath".

This was a word that the Lord had woken Nick up with in the middle of the night about a year earlier. He recalled being woken up abruptly in bed as if to sneeze, but what came out was this word "Zarephath". It was a completely unknown word to him so he enquired of the Lord, and this is what he heard;

"Zarephath – is an ancient smelting place, a hot furnace, where the earth melts, breaks open and gives up its jewels".

Since hearing this Nick hadn't been able to connect it to anywhere - until now.

It turns out there's actually a story in the Bible about a prophet called Elisha who happens to visit an old widow in a town called Zarephath. There was a famine in the land and she was preparing a final meal for herself and her son with last remaining drops of oil - this was going to be their last supper. Into this situation walks the prophet and says, "Make me a cake of bread." Is this just a self centered demand or is he listening to a different voice.... he continues

"Go collect all the containers you can" - she did - and the oil just kept on flowing, filling every vessel - enough for her own needs and plenty to sell.

This was commonly known in those days as a miracle.
And this was our prayer for Caroline.

Dumbartung

On the Wednesday afternoon Gloria's good friend Vanda drove us in to town for an outing to the V&A museum in Perth City, where there was an exhibition of aboriginal art and photography from the turn of the twentieth century. However interesting, the sterile presentation left us feeling dissatisfied - as it told us nothing about the people themselves.

To compensate Gloria made a few calls and a private visit was arranged for us to go to the Dumbartung Aboriginal Corporation. Once inside we were personally shown around the Kyana Cultural Gallery and Keeping Rooms by none other than the founder and curator himself, Robert Eggington.

We were definitely not ready for what we were about to witness, which was in total contrast to the earlier V&A visit.

Robert guided us through an extremely personal tour, which connected us to the stories of Aboriginal people. He talked us through a multitude of artifacts repatriated from around the globe, individual items either stolen or 'acquired' by western private collectors for a pittance. This unscrupulous practice was expanded further in Robert's excellent book 'Hamburgers for Masterpieces' which tells the stories of Aboriginal art created by men and women locked up in prison and how these creatives were tricked into selling their artworks - literally for a burger and chips or a bottle of coca cola.

Already becoming overwhelmed by the scale and quality of the artwork and the personal stories behind each item; we arrived at a pivotal piece situated in the centre of the museum. A large glass cabinet, the size of a man, stared at us - it contained a formal portrait of a modern aboriginal man wearing western clothes.

"What are we seeing"?

Robert quietened...after a very long pause ...his voice cracked with emotion and tears fell from his eyes.
This was his son.
It was a graduation photograph, but also a memorial.

A young man whom, like so many other aboriginal youth, had buckled under the pressures of trying to live in a white world: he had sadly taken his own life.

Our culturally informative and very personal guided tour suddenly swerved in a whole new direction.

We had already been hugely privileged to be given this private tour but now Robert invited us further into Kyana's heart, a private outer room, an intimate place of mourning and healing.

The walls and ceiling of this room were covered with scores of photographs; each one held a brief testimony of loss; teenage young men and women, all aboriginal, all victims of suicide - the room was a space where friends and family could come and mourn, remember, celebrate - and also a place to receive help and support. We begin to get a glimpse into this tragic epidemic of aboriginal teenage suicides.

As we are leaving Robert tells us he doesn't usually bring visitors here, but he'd felt a heart response and thought we'd understand. It was indeed a privilege - a deeply moving one.

The Broken drum...still weeps on.

The question comes again - why are we seeing this, why are these things being revealed to us.
Are we hearing again from the broken drum? We first heard its pounding voice through the Hungarian Holocaust survivor Valerie in 2005, then in 2008 at WCGIP, as indigenous voices sang their laments in Israel and now in 2011 in Perth with Australia's Aborigines?

Since then we've heard it cry out in Lesvos and Calais with refugees drowning in red tape and in the Mediterranean Sea, back on our own doorstep in Rochdale where people live and die on its unforgiving streets; we've even heard the voice of Palestinians clamouring for attention amid bigoted theological correctness.... these are just a few of the worlds' disposable throwaways.

They all cry - will you listen? - Can you hear us?
Can you feel my pain?
Who will help these broken drums sing again?

Robert was a practiced guide and willingly told the story of his people and his family.
Gloria's sister Teresa took us deeper. Teresa was less willing and perhaps rightly less trusting of these two white men she'd only just met. She was also an undoubted doer and clearly raw and smarting from the pain and injustice she was seeing on a daily basis. Teresa worked with troubled aboriginal youth and in particular ran programs for women and girls. If the people were hurting, the youth and women were feeling it particularly in the usual ways: grief and bereavement; sexual violence; domestic abuse; low confidence and close to zero self worth.

Old Drum New Skin

Teresa runs a centre and programs in Armandale for the youth and women aiming to offer a wide range of very practical support but also to increase confidence, strengthen identity and crucially enhance self-esteem. The cycles of violence including that directed against the self, self-harm and suicide must be stopped for the sake of the people, but ultimately for all humanity.
An added privilege was to meet Teresa - another of life's broken drums - who seeks to bring healing to those other drums that encircle her.

The picture we'd been carrying of an old drum needing a new skin gained significance daily as we continued on our journey.

Malcolm & Sharon

Port Kennedy Appointment

About a month before the Corroberee deadline, Nick had a yearning to make four leather pennants to hang on the wooden drum stand; his idea was to inscribe them with Psalm 133 and so he cut the shapes out of a light tan calf hide and finished them off with knotted fringed edges. Once completed he took them around to his friend Sheila Clay who is a dab hand at pyrography (this is a specialized writing/burning technique)

While Sheila was working on the pennants she happened to say "When you go to Perth - could you do me a favour and take some Christmas cards out with you for my friends?"

Nick enthusiastically replied, "Oh I like the sound of that – "When you go to Perth" – "Yes of course I'll take them". It was as if he was receiving a hopeful hook to hang onto.

Sheila went on to tell about her friends, Malcolm and Sharon, who had emigrated from the UK to Port Kennedy a few years earlier; she'd recently heard the disturbing news that Malcolm had just been diagnosed with an aggressive form of brain tumour and the prognosis was not good.

Nick feeling a second surge of urgency said, "This now sounds more like an appointment".

Soon after we arrived in Oz we contacted Sheila's friends to arrange a meeting and deliver the Christmas cards. The only day we had free, turned out to be the Friday...our last day. Gloria, ever the connector, phoned one of her network friends to host us, who just happened to live in a convenient halfway point and so we drove down to Port Kennedy.

Entering the spacious suburban bungalow, we were greeted by our hosts and promptly sat down with Malcolm and Sharon who had already arrived. After a few preliminary 'Hellos' - we completed our postman task of delivering Sheila's Christmas cards; they began sharing the story of their difficult medical journey, which was clearly dominating their thoughts. It was a harrowing tale to hear, particularly considering the hopes they'd come to Australia with and hopes that now seemed to be very short lived and probably about to be dashed.

A quick glance at the clock told us time was moving on and so should we.

Nick felt strongly that we now needed to tell our story and the only real story we had was that of the broken drum. As Nick begins, Dave smiles supportively but inside is thinking "what are you doing Nick, this man has been given a death sentence and all you're offering is a daft story about a broken drum, C'mon we can do better than that".

But Nick...oblivious to Dave's thoughts... Just carries on.

Nick later commented that the drum story was all we had ... he wished we something more...but this is all we've been given to bring...

Towards the end of Nick's telling of the tale he recounts how a week ago we too had reached a desperate place - metaphorically speaking he said....

"We had decorated the nursery - so to speak - got the cot, pram and all the bibs and bobs, in readiness for the expected child of promise...but now it appears we're going to be looking into the face of a still born - Instantly a spirit of hopeless grief fell upon me".

"The dream we'd had - was dead"

Nick spoke directly to Malcolm saying "Sadly Malcolm you know exactly what I'm talking about"

Amazingly Malcolm and Sharon had followed the story closely and seemed to understand how it related to them; they saw themselves in the broken drum story and they could very easily relate to a dream that had died. It also dawned on us that the chance request months earlier to deliver Christmas cards to Sheila's friends was no mere coincidence and that we now felt caught up in some divine conspiracy that had brought us to this appointed time.

Reflecting on how we'd arrived at this point, Nick stated "If it took all of this palaver to travel half way around the world to come and meet you and deliver this crazy story - then it's been worth it – 'cos - God must really love you man.... I think at some point we need to pray... and take the conversation back to 'The Management' - after all, Jesus was the instigator"

For us, looking back, this seems in some small way a shadow of the 'oil mans' bigger story, Jesus leaving His heavenly home to come to earth in order to show us the Father's love.

Our experience of the last week with the drum had taught us that prayer and oil went perfectly together with Psalm 133. However we'd run out of oil and now we needed some.

Nick spotted our hostess in the nearby open plan kitchen, he jumped up and asked her matter of factly if she had any oil.

Old Drum New Skin

"Sunflower or olive?"
"Olive please" replied Nick
"Good" she says, "I've just got a new bottle"
"Great...and have you got a garden and could we use it " asks
Nick as he grabs the bottle.

We're directed to a door near to the kitchen and Dave, Nick,
Malcolm and Sharon exit the house into a beautifully manicured
garden. Outside it's now very hot; forty plus, and our first
thought is to find some shade. Malcolm backs under a tree and
we all follow; bowing our heads to hide from the blistering sun -
mixed with a deepening sense of solemnity. Dave steps into the
leafy shade, looks up and nudges Nick to check out the canopy
covering our impromptu gathering.

What can we see?

It's an olive tree! - Have we been brought to a Gethsemane -
a place of crushing? Gethsemane – a place where olives are
violently pounded to release the golden juice - that they might
produce pure oil for food and lamps to give light.

This relentless olive oil theme stirs up haunting pictures of
Jesus praying in another garden long ago, which bore the name
Gethsemane. The ambush is now getting stronger, as if we were
under heaven's microscope. Everything in creation seems to be
conspiring to bring us to this time and this space.

Nick faces Malcolm and asks him to cup his hands together -
then immediately has second thoughts - saying "No, no put them
down I don't want anything to do with this - this isn't magic - all
we have is oil and the psalm."

As Nick unscrews the olive oil cap his attention is suddenly drawn to his own wedding ring. It bears the Hebrew taken from the 'Song of Songs' love poem: "My beloved is mine and I am His". Straight away his eyes fill up with the weight of this covenantal symbolism and he beckons Sharon closer saying "You need to be here too, this is about both of you guys not just Malcolm. We are only here to support you." Nick lifts the bottle up high to the Creator and begins to pour the oil as he speaks out the beautiful words of Psalm 133.

The oil falls unhindered through the air onto the dry ground - the arid soil immediately drinks it up as if creation too wants to receive a blessing At some point Malcolm intuitively lifts up his hands to catch the streaming oil, Sharon sees his gesture and moves closer, cupping her tiny fingers beneath his.

What a heartrending picture of undying love.
Eventually the flow of oil ceased.

We stood still - caught in the dreaminess - savouring this precious moment

Sharon tenderly broke the delicate silence asking Malcolm "are you ok?"
Malcolm softly exhaled "I'm... err...ok.... feel quite emotional"
Sharon replied "I know I was nearly going too... I get like this at church - but I stop myself - and hold it back "
Nick interrupts "but why - they — we - we need to see and be affected by your tears —
Hey these tears they're not just given for you, you know"

Sharon sighed, "I know but I'm holding back for..."
It was like she was about to say "for when the inevitable happens ".

Again Nick pre-empts and wades in "Who says that its going to be inevitable...I'm not saying kiss your brains goodbye...yes you need to listen to your physicians...but the Lord wants to be in on this conversation too - Hey a week ago all this Oz thing had utterly died for us then 'He' resurrected it and we haven't stopped dreaming since."

With that final declaration of dreamy hope - the four of us fell into a joyous thanksgiving hug - mixed with laughter, tears and a strange sense of release.

All too soon, time had run out and the four of us needed to reluctantly return to the worlds' Chronos time and get back on the road; tears were wiped, belongings gathered and a quick agreement made to keep in touch. They headed home and we were on our way north for our final evening in Perth.

Looking back on these blissful, yet fleeting moments, one would think that we would've at least prayed for Malcolm to be healed! Its true, but to be perfectly honest, in all the oily euphoria, it sort of slipped our thoughts. It was as if we had been caught up in the Creator's river of dreams. Nevertheless intercession was birthed here, as we were included into a blessed river of unifying prayer, flowing with family and friends for Malcolm, until October 2015 when his long and courageous battle was finally over.

Why?
The Gospels tell us that Jesus Himself was hard-pressed to ask an extremely needy question from his disciples "Will you watch with me?". Agonising words cried out in a garden ambiguously known as Gethsemane, because this is not the beauty spot we are often presented with.

So let us not be too quick to separate the earthly from the divine, for in our own dark Gethsemane's we too may encounter an unexpected connection with the great mystery that Christ de-mystifies for those drawn into the fellowship of his sufferings.

Either directly or indirectly by the unspoken broken spirit, we may also be called upon by individuals to 'watch with them' as they pass through dark nights and days of the soul.

I suspect that this is what was happening as the blistering sun helped us seek shelter under that olive tree in a back garden in Australia. A task none of us could have predicted or prepared for, but one we were so privileged to have been invited into.

Last Night of the Poms

Finally we arrived at our last night in Perth and expectations were set at super high following such a 'totally off the SatNav charts' kind of week. Especially, since tonight we are visiting an Aboriginal church and our thinking is that it will be much freer and less inhibited amongst our indigenous friends.

The attendance was relatively low but by this time we were getting used to Abba's curious ways of working; as the good book says 'where 2 or 3 gathered in my name - there I AM - in the midst'; small groups and even one to one`s are no barrier to the Creator showing His hand.

Nonetheless we hadn't anticipated yet another ambush, this time a sobering kickback from an unexpected institutional mindset.

The night was like any other Friday night church meeting – but this one had more than its fair share of underlying agendas circulating in the room, and some of the individuals present held very rigid views - like buckled-down straight jackets in pews – fixed ideas on what a 'meeting' should include or how God might manifest Himself; and it wasn't long before the dissent was vocalized.

It was during the time of `praise and worship' that several individuals willfully stood up and began venting their displeasure

with shouts of;
> "Is this all we're going to be doing all night"
> "What about reading the Word."

We were shocked and Gloria became visibly and verbally angry at the affront, confronting the individuals with a stinging challenge.

"This last week we have seen the Lord literally pour out blessing after unexpected blessing as we've been obedient to Him - to play the drum, pour the oil and sing the psalm - tonight is the summit – so we've brought it here to share with you – but if you don't want it - that's fair enough - we will take it elsewhere".

Her words cut deep - immediately several more people exited the building - somewhat thinning the already sparse crowd – so we decided to come down from the staged worship area and continue the conversation sat alongside the few who remained. Seated closer we began to share, much more freely and informally now, some of the highlights of our week - specifically referring to the drum, Psalm 133 and the oil. We also touched on key themes of this psalms blessing to bring about repentance, reconciliation and healing; healing for the land as well as for its people. On hearing this several more folks decide to steal away, leaving a smaller but more receptive remnant.

It was time to cease the yarning and start the pouring – and once again the recurring theme of the great outdoors beckoned.

So the seven of us (good number) strolled outside into the parking lot and stood expectantly on the grass verge, as a fresh 4-litre can of the finest virgin olive oil was uncapped. And we began to proclaim the now familiar psalm of unity accompanied by the glug, glug, glug of olive oil into eagerly cupped hands - which effortlessly seeped its way through our fingers - falling like precious rain onto the parched earth. The sight of this double blessing - "for the people and their land" - reinvigorated us into much deeper prayer.

Then, right out of the proverbial blue, Gloria jumps into the centre of the group and declares;

"Well if others choose to reject His blessing ....I don't want to miss out...I want it all...I want everything that God has got for me".

She then humbly bowed her upper body , hanging her head over - inviting us to deluge her with whatever was left in the can (approximately 3 litres); as the oil gushes over our Aboriginal sister the level of joy in our small gathering was giddily stepped up to a whole new dimension.

Gloria drank in the anointing - heartily absorbing it - like a sponge, into her glowing spirit as well as her clothing; she arose like a leviathan from the deep - flailing the airwaves, twirling her oil soaked hair.

This was such a fitting ending to our last evening – and a totally apt benediction to an "off the charts" dreamy week of doing things the Lord's way.

We laughed and laughed...great belly laughs filled with incomprehensible wonderment...all we needed now was a cheeseburger and fries and Gloria lead the way into the diner - dripping a trail of sanctified oil behind her, saying: "Job well done lads...cycle complete!"

After word

Hindsight is a most wonderful thing. Like peering in a rear view mirror, it exists to help us make sense out of what has taken place.

This is how cathartic the process of writing ODNS has been for us...having taken nine years to travel down the road, before we could begin to focus on what had actually happened.

Its fair to say that when we first set out on this journey, we thought it was just going to be a simple story about a couple of drums - one old and one new - then serendipitously it fast became something far more involved – vastly stretching our previously known spiritual boundaries, challenging our willingness to step out into the unknown, especially when it touched our wallets. ...Making them squeal. But this is precisely what tends to happen when you pursue the " Divine Management's Directions"... things change dramatically, "simply coz" it's a way we've never ventured before!

Initially the drum story proved to be a really good hook that inspired us to write and record a brand new song entitled "Old Drum New Skin" - then spookily we began to recognize the individuals spoken of in the lyrics? Like late developers it took us quite a while to realise that the "Old broken Drum" actually represented the broken-hearted stories sung by those we would meet on our listening journeys.

On one such outing Nick met a remarkable Romanian lady called Doină, who turned out to be a key liberator of a cruel orphanage hidden away from probing eyes. He was intrigued to find out what her name meant – her reply was not at all what he was expecting – she explained; "in my language it describes a person who sings sad songs." Her explanation absolutely floored him as it tenderly conveyed what she had done for these poor discarded children. Her name also prompted Nick to remember the fabulous jazz singer Billie Holliday, who was affectionately known as the "Lady who sings the Blues"; such titles aptly describe the weight that these people carried.

As we recall the folks we've recently met we can never forget the first person that pierced our souls back in 2005. She was an astonishing woman who unlocked a door into a previously unknown world. It was in her tiny bed-sit apartment that we began to hear the harrowing voices emanating from these "portals of pain". We speak of our Jewish friend Valerie Juhasz who not only miraculously survived being murdered in the gas chambers of Auschwitz, but outlived the infamous "death march". This seemingly chance encounter in Jerusalem, kick-started our entry into being videographers, the result was the docudrama "Valerie's Orchard" (available to view on our website www.breakspearinc.com/film/).

To be clear, we are not professional video-counselors holding scheduled therapy sessions. No, these were merely ordinary folks we happened to meet on life's not so normal crazy journey; our paths just crossed - as if the great cross-bearer 'Himself' wanted them too! So that he could ask his piercing questions -
Can you feel my pain?
Will you be my ears...my arms of comfort?
Will you be a voice for the voiceless?

The powerless silent screamers
The suspects, under surveillance
The driven out - of house, home and lands
Those excluded from loving-kindness
Unseen – overlooked by design
Those on the edge – and those being pushed way beyond it

They are the outsiders looking into the bread shop windows with no money to buy.

The more you look, the more you see; the sad stories are utterly endless, exceeded only by the cross-bearers healing antidote.

Listening to these diabolical revelations proved to be a real eye-opener into the burdensome power of memory, especially when it hasn't been amicably resolved, escalating into subsequent generations, and potentially building up a head of steam for a perfect eruption. They also point to the desperate need for remembering – and to be remembered.

Maybe this is what the "end of days" reckoning is going to look like - a book of deeds done or not done – sins of omission – or sins of commission? What have we done - for the least of these my friends? What have we done – for the least of these – His friends?

We've equated the recurring theme of the "Old Broken Drum" to an olive press or to put it another way "a Gethsemane experience" - a dark night of the soul - where the olives are selected, gathered and brutally crushed in order to release the precious golden juice of their broken story. This for many individuals is a very costly and personal offering - even though at the time they do not comprehend it!

These images are shockingly reminiscent of Jesus' own harrowing journey into a garden called Gethsemane, which incidentally is the `Aramaic' word to describe an olive press or a fruit crusher. It was here in this symbolically charged place that His spirit was excruciatingly compressed in prayer - the very night before his own agonizing death. Oh what an incredible unsanitized insight we have been given (in the disciples account)

- into the divine identification with the plight of the earthly suffering soul.

So why should we be drawn by such an inanimate object as an old broken drum to express man's painful narrative? - be it past, present or even future woes. For us as drummers the voice of the drum speaks profoundly, like the native "talking drums" of Africa, which are used to great effect to communicate important messages through the airwaves - to those who have ears to receive.

The Divine both speaks and listens through a whole host of languages, not all of them human. To this end we have begun to hear and learn a new heart language, listening, translating and playing what we have heard into healing prayers. Sometimes these are not pretty or well-rounded petitions but desperate thorny heartbeats launched heavenward to an attentive Creator who listens to broken people - tormented by wounded memories – played out...prayed out on an old drum - with a new skin.

The purest oil is created for the highest purpose
To bring light into the darkness
There it burns as a beacon of hope
Illuminating a very different way to tread
With the promise that joy... Will come
.... In the morning

May the "Do Good" heartbeat play on...do good...do good...do good

Old Drum
New Skin
Gallery

Gallery Photos

KAAL CORROBOREE
Fan the Flames 2011
International Gathering

Partnership
Participation
Learn
Experience
Encourage

21st - 27th November, 2011
PERTH, WESTERN AUSTRALIA

Breakspear

UK based Breakspear Inc **will be presenting their latest work** *Old Drum New Skin* **at the KAAL Corroboree.**

The band are thrilled to be joined on stage by local and international guest artists, making for an exciting and vibrant festival lineup.

For over a decade Nick Breakspear has headed up the Breakspear *Performance Art Ensemble* a global touring company made up of fluid members, working predominantly in the area of conceptual music, drawing on the rich Judeo / Christian 'Mystery Plays' of old - resulting in their own take on modern day parables - heavenly pictures painted on earth with a contemporary zesty twist!

They're Like Pizza With Everything On!
NEW YORK DRUMMER - JOEY BRENNAN

Never to be pigeon-holed, the Breakspear brew has enjoyed fusing Rock, Jazz, Funk, Blues, Gospel, Hip Hop - in fact any available genre for their current lyrics. Nick says *"it was never just about the music, but sourcing Jesus particular brand of righteous Love and justice in our hurting world"*

Working out these awkward life questions has lead to the creation of some funky theatrical presentations and more recently venturing into the world of film.

Breakspear Inc.
(Above Left to right) Dave Baker, Prem Joseph, Nick Breakspear Andy Green and Dave Woodman

Filming at WCGIP (Jerusalem 2008)
(Left to right) Nick Breakspear, Paul O'toko, Paul Coppack and Dave Baker

The guys will be premiering their latest creation *Old Drum New Skin* a contemporary metaphorical parable, based on the elusive gift of unity – spoken of by the psalmists of yore, the presentation will include a short film based on the journey of *Gloria* an Aboriginal lady who's travels took her to the remote atolls of Vanuatu in the South Pacific, then all the way up to us guys in the Northern Hemisphere carrying a mysterious and prophetic stone.

Intrigued - so are we – see you there!

Breakspear's music
www.valeriesorchard.com/nick-music

Performing at Panim El Panim UK (2010)
(Left to right) Nick Breakspear and Dave Woodman

Thanks...

Nick and Dave have been travelling together for the best part of fifteen years, on what have become known as the Breakspear Inc projects; or 'Inc' for short.

The Inc is an umbrella term which denotes those individuals who have responded to invitations to be 'included' into our little family of creative playmates. Sometimes they contribute for a season to help paint a specific picture the Creator wants us to create. Some have even ended up staying on as permanent sojourners.

A note from Nick

These ventures are only made possible through consistently tuning into the Creator's dream channel. Along with unceasing encouragement from my beloved wife Anni and family who not only support me, but send me out as a taproot to pursue heavenly visions, that I may return with tales to tell of the quest.

A note from Dave

I am very grateful to all of my friends and family for their encouragement, mixed with just enough curiosity, and a morsel of bewilderment; kind listening questions. Special thanks to my wife Sharon for her patience and the timely impetus to 'do something'.

Special Thanks

We would like to thank all those who supported this endeavor, even though it was a little off the wall.

Film Crew Paul 'Cop' Coppack, Kath McArragher & Paul 'Sparx' Sparkes @ Shooters Media

The Band David Woodman, Andy Green, Prem Joseph, Frank Brierley & Phil Jones

UK & Down Under
Gloria Miller & her Noongyar community, especially her sister Teresa and Vanda Ramsay, along with brother Warren and the PNG mob
David Clements for waking us up
Sheila Clay for her pyrography and Christmas cards
Malcolm & Sharon
The folks of Dwelling Up
Caroline Margaret River
Robert Eggington
Helen Anderson
Anni & Abigail for airport transfers
Karen Lowe & Deborah Chapman - Antioch Church, Llanelli, Wales
Steve & Issie Smith, Cardiff
Helen, London
Port Kennedy Friends
The House of John wet-mob-dancers Blackstone Edge for the front and back cover photos
and finally a huge thanks to Pilgrim Designs for helping us to finally get this print on the page